wonderful cities of
ITALY

WHITE STAR
PUBLISHERS

Photographs
Marcello Bertinetti
Giulio Veggi

Introduction
Piero Bairati

Editorial coordination
Valeria Manferto De Fabianis

Translation
Richard Reville

© 1990, 2003 White Star S.r.l.
Via C. Sassone, 22/24
13100 Vercelli, Italy - www.whitestar.it

ISBN 88-8095-848-8

Reprints:
2 3 4 5 6   09 08 07 06 05

Printed in Thailand

Page 1

Venice: the Serenissima's winged lion.

Pages 2-3

Turin: view of city center.

Pages 4-5

Venice: Church of Santa Maria della Salute.

Pages 6-7

Milan: Galleria in Corso Vittorio Emanuele.

Pages 8-9

Rome: Roman Forum.

Page 10

Venice: Church of San Giorgio Maggiore.

Page 11

Genoa: Porta Soprana.

CONTENTS

Preface

The unification of Europe is moving toward completion, or at least, that is what television and the press tell us every day. This, in fact, means only that common rules increasingly regulate the exchange of goods and services, the movement of capital and men, the payment of the taxes, and Europe s economic and political relationships with the rest of the world. There is far less use of customs and passports.

That is enough for us: indeed, we can desire no more. This unification represents a measure of uniformity that guarantees our continent s compactness and strength, while leaving our historical distinctions and the peculiarities of civic and cultural life intact. To a great extent, we have a single market, a single currency, and a measure of political unity.

But, we must ask ourselves how much will we continue to enjoy that disorganized multiplicity, that anarchy of spirit, which has

always characterized European history, even in those moments when hegemonic designs seemed to be on the point of becoming reality.

It would be anachronistic to fear that the process of European integration will tend to make us more homogeneous. In any case, any such effect would not turn out to be stronger or more worrying than those brought about by the economic and social model we have chosen and under which we are happy to live.

However, if we had to decide whether there was a dividing line, a historical barrier capable of contrasting past and present and the processes of greater uniformity that characterize our era, then this volume of photographs would give us, if not an answer, at least, grounds for reflection.

Cities, with their historic centers, their stratifications of cultures and passions, their buildings, facilities, and squares organized in long-lasting geometric shapes, continue to transmit their own messages, strongly characterized by their recognized language and grammar.

While the contemporary economy asserts itself through increasingly standardized consumption and penetration into apparently very different societies, the city (almost by definition the privileged site of modernization) continues to be an individual: a specific, indomitable, sometimes refractory historical reality.

The city has managed to withstand everything: monarchies and republics, dictatorships and democracies; Florence and Rome even survived the passage of the Savoy dynasty. The city also manages to stand up to the impact of social and political revolutions (Turin, Milan and Genoa survived industrialization, the economic miracle, and neo-capitalism). In time, the city absorbs the conflicts and divisions that it produces.

Cities attract wealth, display it, multiply it and conceal it: the medium-sized cities (Italy s wealthiest) are an eloquent example of this. However, the city also attracts poverty, which buries and institutionalizes itself in specific quarters. Every large or medium city has an underside verging on horror: every aspect of modernity has the third world at its heels.

The city is not made of wax and does not limit itself to recording passively its own historical experience in a book of memoirs. No, the city is not such a book; rather, it is a compilation of successive pages, each of a different character. Because of their historical character, this seems to be the vocation of European cities: to enter into and play in creative tension with the changes in society and institutions.

Almost all modern European cities were founded or rebuilt in the Middle Ages.

There are few exceptions: Renaissance or Baroque cities (built on the initiative of the state as fortified cities, state capitals, naval bases, or for the mere whim of a prince), a certain number of bathing resorts, and a few urban centers created by totalitarian regimes. Apart from these minor anomalies, the European urban system has ancient bones. While medieval city development extended the network of European settlements, it more often built on top of previous construction, on more or less consistent Roman remains, Celtic structures or Iron Age residues.

The network that connects Italian cities does not have such a narrow mesh as the German network has. This latter developed over the course of the centuries from different waves of urbanization, creating a compact connective tissue, one which compensates, to a certain extent, for Germany s long fragmentation under the rule of the Holy Roman Empire. Political barriers have never canceled this network, which the now strengthening German reunification is restoring to a new functionality.

The Italian urban system does not even carry clear and omnipresent signs of the uniformity-promoting force of central state administration and the different wills to power which have been recurrent in the history of France, that land of revolution and weighty bureaucracies, peremptory metropolitan hegemonies and a very determined centralism. On the other hand, the Italian city seems to have grown on itself.

The history of Italy, as Carlo Cattaneo s teachings claim, is, above all, the history of its cities.

Pages 13-14

Cagliari: sunset over the old city.

Italian cities have conserved traces of every epoch, signs or complete architectural and urban styles, distinguishable but often tainted by a single irrecoverable color. Carducci, when he discovered he was an urban poet, also taught us how to observe the world of the city through the medium of color. Joseph Toth went even further, looking for the infancy of Europe in the white cities of Provence. Palermo is pink. Bari is white. Rome is a golden yellow. Florence is green and silvery. Bologna is red. Venice is an inexhaustible source of greens. Milan is gray and red. Turin grayish green. As an essential ingredient of the urban language and the messages sent out by the city, color also becomes an integral part of the stereotype, that particular symbol by which a city is identified. Color is a metaphor of a city s history, sometimes irritating, arbitrary, vulgarly didactic, but also inevitable, unexceptional, and the trigger of automatic recognition.

known, neglecting the rest or paying only superficial attention to it.

This is how things stand in theory. Or rather, they would be like that in a society in which citizens did not have a lot of images at their disposal. In these conditions, the postcard, the painting or drawing commissioned by the tourist from the street artist, the production of touristic-landscape-monumental kitsch and the holiday snap would constitute the exclusive or widely prevalent source of visual culture. But we know that things are not like that.

In our life as citizens of this period in the century, our perceptive zones are bombarded, not infrequently to our pleasure, by an almost uninterrupted series of images. Our "seen" patrimony has now acquired a capacity for unprecedented quantitative increase and qualitative change. We pass a thousand times across the gigantic spaces and forms of Milan s Central Station without thinking even for a moment about their eventual artistic

In the course of the TV news, a photograph of Turin s Mole Antonelliana provides the backdrop for an item about the motor industry; Bologna s two towers or Milan s Madonnina and the Duomo s spires highlight the anniversary of massacres and other events linked to terrorism. A city s color and its symbol thus gain a conspicuous position in our collective visual culture: indeed, they have become permanent structures.

An entire city delegates its symbolic representation to a blue-ribbon monument or to a complex of urbanistic-architectonic structures with a strong emblematic value. It has been observed that the constitution and use of the stereotype is a reduction, in minimal terms, of the richness of the city. Once Milan becomes the Cathedral, Pisa, the Leaning Tower, Venice, the Rialto Bridge, etc., tourists will head toward these objects which are already part of their visual patrimony and they re-appropriate the already

significance. We treat them like cast-off clothes, until the day when a restoration or a talented photographer manages to penetrate our distraction and open up a new horizon in our perception of a cityscape.

We have also learned fear: investigations into architectural and urban pathologies (no thanks to the diligence of the public administration) have made us familiar with wrinkles and erosions, cracks and fractures which at one time would have escaped the attention of the common observer—and even of that of the those whose job it is to see them.

The heightening of our capacity to observe the city more closely, the improvement of other instruments for the observation and control of the urban heritage, renders even more scandalous the collapses, decay, and ruins which we have seen and are still forced to countenance in our cities; even though, when faced with this we cannot fail to recognize that now we have a finer perception of urban reality. The unlimited possibility of producing images has substantially changed our rapport with the city. Not only do we have a more powerful magnifying glass on the urban world at our disposition; we also dispose of the possibility of verifying or falsifying our representations and our visual schemes. In the urban phenomenon we live and change the city and we are changed by living there. Heraclitus of Ephesus, a philosopher saddened by the mutilations and contradictions of reality, would perhaps be enthusiastic or at least comforted to live in our extraordinary flow of visions.

In these conditions, the stereotype, while still surviving, must come to terms with an accelerated production of representations that constantly put it under discussion. Photography, in all its possible meanings and forms of expression, has the function of constantly re-qualifying our visual code. The production of images of the city has become an almost nonstop activity.

Keeping us in direct contact with the spaces, the masses, the horizons of the urban world, in the detail and peculiarity of their history, in their transformation according to the rules of a deep language, the flow of urban images does not do anything but build and rebuild the structures of our visual knowledge.

The revitalization of our iconographic patrimony and the requalification of the perceptive structures through which these images find a place in our mental baggage, in our internal theater (the city too is theater and memory) correspond to a primeval need.

The towers of San Gimignano, the fortress of San Leo Castel del Monte, Buon Consiglio, Via San Leonardo, Piazza dei Miracoli, Ascoli s Piazza del Popolo, in this very fertile Heraclitian culture in which we have the privilege of living, can and must be photographed and seen thousands of times, without being worn down, without satisfying the need of our eyes to see them, without suppressing in our visual memory the need for other visitations.

If living in the flow of images and growing in the school they provide produces a slow erosion of stereotypes, then the heightening of our capacity to experiment with and read the urban phenomenon has contributed to render less rigid the concept of "planning."

Removed from the bureaucratic and administrative sphere, the "plan" has come to signify a dynamic process of successive superimpositions and experiences, an accumulation of functions, not only the more or less rational sum of planimetries. The city is not only a book, but also means a complex bundle of institutions, hierarchies and roles. The most silent ecologist has patented and monopolized the notion of "complexity."

In reality this has a centuries -long history, so much so, indeed, that it can be identified with the long past of the medieval and modern city.

Indeed, a purely formalistic vision of the "plan," especially when it leads us to consider the chessboard as the most natural form for a city, would not even help to interpret the urban history of antiquity.

It would immediately make a distinction between cities that were "founded," created by a central planning force, and cities that grew in a presumed surge of spontaneity. In the depths of the Etruscan cities and in the original urban layers of that sort of America which was Sicily in the 6th century B.C., as well as in the innumerable Roman military camps which gave soul to many Italian cities, we will certainly find the orderly chessboard. But the story of urbanism in antiquity teaches us that the same chessboard can have different meanings: it can be linked to a cosmogonical conception and might have the streets laid out according to the cardinal points, the ownership of the land or according to the distribution of political, religious and military structures.

"Complexity" seems to characterize the structure of the city right from its origins and throughout its history up to our days. If this concept is valid in correcting the unilaterality of geometry, it also places precise limitations on the presumed spontaneity of growth. An apparently disordered city like Siena reveals a superb coordination of nuclei and functions along the nervature of Piazza del Campo.

It is not possible, from these difficult equilibria, to extract an encouraging message.

The Italian city manages however to transmit a sense of pride, a will for independence, a capacity to produce modernity and to resist it according to a logic which is recognizable in its history.

Page 14
Siena, city center.

Page 15
Lucca: Piazza del Mercato and the Church of San Michele.

Pages 16-17
Bari: aerial view of the city.

Pages 18-19
Florence: Ponte Vecchio.

Page 20 top

Palermo: the equestrian group which surmounts the Politeama Garibaldi Theater.

Page 20 bottom

Naples: the Church of San Francesco di Paola.

Page 21

Pisa: sunset over the Lungoamo.

City of art
of history
# of culture

Even a cultured Italian will find it difficult to choose an ideal itinerary for a friend ...

GIOVANNI ARPINO

Rome
The challenge of time

Nightfall is one of the most fascinating moments in the capital. Seen from above, the city seems to dissolve into the dusk, for a moment losing its boundaries, before spreading endlessly into the distance as the lights come on in the streets, squares, narrow alleyways, and in the timeworn houses. This is an added enchantment, a skillful spell that Rome casts to assert her undeniable and multi-layered beauty against the ravages of time.

Page 22 top
The uncertain glow of the torch flames creates alluring plays of light around one of the statues that adorn the façade of the Campidoglio.

Page 22 bottom
Sunset's golden light touches and highlights the exquisite perfection of the mosaics in the loggia of Santa Maria Maggiore.

Page 23 top
The statues of the Dioscuri frame the entrance to the Campidoglio, festively illuminated on 21 April, anniversary Rome's foundation.

Pages 22-23
The Fiume fountain's mythical figures seem to come almost disquietingly to life, drawing vitality and movement from the light reflected on the water's surface.

Pages 24-25
The world-famous Trevi Fountain, the work of Nicola Salvi, is a masterpiece of Baroque art. At its center is Oceanus driving a carriage drawn by two horses and two Tritons.

Pages 26-27
Construction of the Coliseum was begun under Vespasian in 70 A.D. and was completed c. 150 A.D. under Titus. The Flavian Amphitheater, designed for public performances and gladiator fights, could hold more than 50,000 people.

Page 28 top

A charming detail of one of the four statues that decorate Bernini's Fontane dei Fiumi, in Piazza Navona.

Page 28 right

The ten statues of angels that embellish Ponte Sant'Angelo date from 1666; they reflect Bernini's genius.

Page 29

The dynamic equestrian statues of the Dioscuri flank the flight of stairs in Piazza Campidoglio.

Every historical monument has been documented, studied, analyzed and subjected to the judgment of critics, discussed and re-discussed. The influence that Rome has had on the development of European civilization is inestimable and endures, albeit in a different manner, even today. It is precisely from such a position of hegemony that the city obtains that inner security which enables it to overcome the problems which derive from the rhythms and demands of present-day life. With extraordinary stubbornness Rome rises above contingent human precariousness to re-propose itself with renewed vigor as the only true Eternal City.

Pages 30-31
A still sleepy city welcomes the first rays of the rising sun.

Page 31 left
Palazzo Chigi, official residence of the Premier, was built on the orders of Pope Alexander VII for his family's use.

Rome's people represent an inestimable wealth within the city's heritage. They live in an urban environment and breathe a cosmopolitan atmosphere amid the most prestigious figures in international politics and culture, yet Romans have managed to conserve and pass on the traditional customs of working-class civilization; ancient traditions which are perpetuated through everyday gestures and habits. Thanks to its extraordinary population, Rome has managed escape the fate of modern metropolises and maintain intact its authentic character and original historical, social and cultural significance.

Pages 34-35
The Spanish Steps in Piazza di Spagna are one of the favorite meeting places for the young people of Rome. They date from 1792 and are dominated by the Church of SS Trinità dei Monti, erected in 1485, and by an imposing obelisk found in the Gardens of Sallust.

The pageant provided by St. Peter's Square on the occasion of the Pope's Easter blessing "Urbi et Orbi" and on other solemn ceremonies and celebrations is truly impressive. A crowd of more than 200,000 throng the enormous ellipse in a unique and unifying act of faith.

Pages 38-39
In Spring night descends sedately over the city, cloaking it with delicate shades of color.

Milan
The rampant
metropolis

The Duomo, Italy's largest Gothic structure, is Milan's principal monument. Construction began under Gian Galeazzo Visconti in 1386, but the architect's name is lost to history. In the early years, French and German masters alternately directed the work, which continued until 1500. In 1769, the spire surmounted by the Madonnina was built above the lantern. The façade was completed at the beginning of the 19th century, and the numerous spires were all completed by 1887.

Pages 40-41

More than 2000 statues enliven the Duomo's sides and pinnacles: the surge of its slender lines terminates in a confusion of 135 spires. The largest spire, above the central lantern, is surmounted by a gilded statue of the Madonna.

Pages 42-43

Piazza Duomo is Milan's geometrical center. The equestrian statue of Vittorio Emanuele II was erected in 1896.

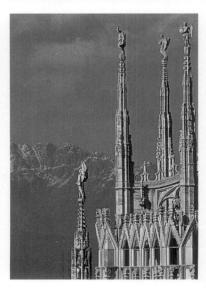

Modern Milan's origins date back to the beginning of the 18th century. The city adorned itself with noble neo-classical buildings and, after the unification of Italy, continued to develop with a crescendo of initiatives and activities, profoundly changing its appearance until it became the metropolis it is today. Milan's city plan is star-shaped, with the Piazza Duomo at its center. The Naviglio, the ancient circular navigable canal, marked the limit of the medieval zone. A second ring, formed by boulevards laid out after the Spanish bastions were demolished, encloses the area within which Milan's most vibrant social life takes place.

Top

The Roman colonnade in the basilica of San Lorenzo Maggiore captures the splendor of Mediolanum (Milan), at one time the capital of the Roman Empire.

Right

The church of Santa Maria delle Grazie, attributed to Donato Bramante, is one of the loveliest of Milan's sacred buildings.

Page 45

An unusual modern bust stands out against the church of Santa Maria del Carmine.

Pages 46-47

At night a dazzling array of twinkling lights illuminates Milan.

Pages 48-49
By day, multicolored crowds fill the Corso Vittorio Emanuele's arcades, attracted to the high-quality shops.

Page 48 top
The Bagutta restaurant was once a painters and artists' meeting place; today show-business and art-world personalities seek an exclusive atmosphere there.

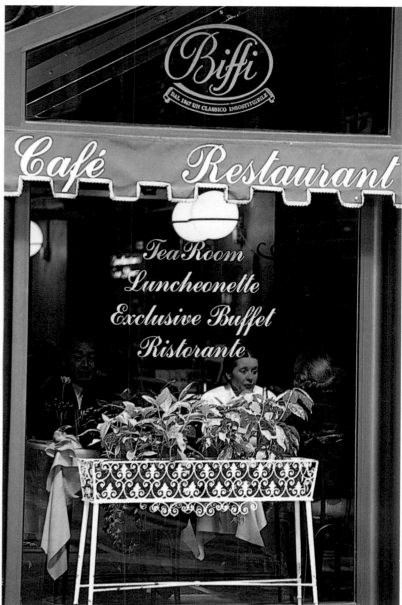

Page 49
At the end of the last century, Café Biffi was a favorite meeting place for Milan's Bohemians and intellectuals. Today, an elegant, cosmopolitan atmosphere reigns supreme.

Left

Milan is famous for art in all its forms: its many galleries enjoy high renown.

Top right

An antiques' shop in the city center. Antique or modern, the art Milan offers connoisseurs is of the highest quality.

Pages 50-51

Over the last few decades, Milan has established itself as a leader in international fashion.

Page 51 top left and right

Via della Spiga (left) and Via Santo Spirito are world-famous names in Milan's fashion center.

Pages 52-53

Built by Giuseppe Piermarini in 1778, on the site of Santa Maria della Scala (from which it takes its name), La Scala is perhaps the world's most famous opera house.

Galleria Vittorio Emanuele, which connects Piazza del Duomo and Piazza della Scala, was built between 1865 and 1877, under the capable guidance of architect Giuseppe Mengoni. Slender iron structures support glass vaults that illuminate the Galleria with vivid azurean light, and the mosaics on the floor present a wide range of polychromatic designs. The Galleria's high-class shops, bookshops, cafés and restaurants make it a draw for the Milanese and for visitors.

Page 57 top left
The imposing bulk of the Arco della Pace (Arch of Peace) stands at the end of Corso Sempione.

Pages 57 top center
center The Sforzesco Castle is, without doubt, the city's most significant example of civic architecture.

Page 57 top right
Like all cities, Milan takes on a completely different appearance with the return of Spring.

Page 56
Castello Sforzesco was built by Francesco Sforza on the 14th-century ruins of the Visconti fortress.

Pages 56-57
Every year, in December, Piazza Sant'Ambrogio comes alive with the voices and colors of the traditional fair of the "Oh bei, Oh bei."

Varese
itinerary among the villas

Pages 58-59
The lovely bell-tower of the Basilica of San Vittore stands out in the panorama of Varese.

Page 59 top left
Palazzo Estense, built by Francesco III d'Este, now serves as Varese's Town Hall.

Page 59 top right
Villa Mirabello, situated in a delightful corner of an Italian garden, now houses the Civic Museums.

Pages 60-61
Evening shadows descend over the Sacro Monte.

Bergamo
under a sky of cupolas

For someone arriving from the plain, Bergamo offers a charming sight with its Upper City dominating the hill. The Upper City's twisting, silent streets still project something of the atmosphere of a medieval city and its Piazza Vecchia and adjacent Piazza del Duomo contain many interesting monuments. In the 19th century and in the early years of the 20th, academics and intellectuals mixed with eccentrics and odd characters in the historic Caffè del Tasso, which still conserves the characteristic atmosphere of its past.

Protected by a solid ring of 16th-century walls, Bergamo rises up with an intact array of cupolas, spires, and bell-towers. Priceless buildings in the Gothic and Baroque styles mingle with others dating from the Middle Ages and the Renaissance. The Romanesque church of Santa Maria Maggiore and the Cathedral form a single complex with their play of cupolas and bell-towers. The interior of Santa Maria Maggiore, famous for its magnificent stuccoes and gilding, was restored in the 16th and 17th centuries. Light beams flooding in from fenestrated cupolas create blinding chromatic patterns as they reflect off the costly decorative elements.

**Como
the city on the golden
lake**

Pages 66-67 top

In Como, life's moments of rest and pleasure are enjoyed on the Lungo Lario.

Pages 66-67 bottom

Villa Olmo is a large Neo-Classic building situated at the center of a splendid park, now open to the public. Its handsome salons host exhibitions, congresses and concerts.

Page 67

In the pinkish light of the setting sun, the rack-railway climbs up to the wooded plateau on which Brunate is situated. Below a picturesque panorama extends.

Como is in a valley that opens onto the lake. The vibrant modern town is a lively tourist center, offering both fine cultural attractions and also a splendid natural setting. Attractions include sailing regattas, motorboat racing, and rowing competitions as well as a prestigious concert season, ballets and art exhibitions. Como is also an unmatched location for conventions and congresses, with a lakefront dotted with elegant bars with open-air terraces.

Page 68
Night-time illuminations are reflected in the water of the lake. Visible in the background is the Neo-Classic form of the Tempio Voltiano, erected in 1927 to honor the centenary of the birth of Alessandro Volta. Villa Olmo can be seen in the distance.

Page 69
Summer sunsets offer memorable images: while the mountains slip into shadow, the city and the lake glow with quivering light. Monuments, villas, parks, bars and landing stages all light up Como's night life.

Mantua
Pearl of the
Renaissance

Mantua was just a small rural center in 70 B.C., when the great Roman poet Virgil was born nearby. It began to flourish during the period of the Free Cities and continued to do so under the Gonzaga family's rule. During the 15th and 16th centuries Mantua's political importance and economic prosperity grew enormously and it became a lead- ing center of Renaissance arts and culture. The court became one of the most sumptuous of Europe and, especially under Isabelle d'Este, gave hospitality to many artists and men of let- ters. Of these Mantegna, Leon Battista Alberti and Giulio Romano have left in Mantua substantial evidence of their genius.

Page 70

Top left Palazzo Te, the grandiose vil- la of the Gonzagas designed by Giulio Romano.

Page 70

Top right Piazza Sordello has main- tained its medieval appearance. It is surrounded by 17th-century crenel- lated buildings, above which rises the Torre della Gabbia. Visible in the background is the cupola of the Church of Sant'Andrea, designed by Juvarra.

Page 71

The Palazzo dei Capitani is one of the oldest buildings which make up the Palazzo Ducale, itself of great interest because of its internal decoration and its art collection.

The tranquil city streets, the numerous mansions and houses built in the typical architectural style of the Po plain, the rich tonality of the colors, the lake and the Rio all represent features of indubitable charm. Mantua is a silent city and the splendor of its ducal past emerges with dignified nobility from every building in its historic center. The city has conserved its human dimension and preserved its antique layout against the invasion of industrial settlements; these are confined to the far side of the lakes.

Turin the capital of Savoy

Turin, the ancient Augusta Taurinorum, acquired importance with the rise of the House of Savoy, which in the 13th century made it the capital of its state. It was then that transformation of the city began, not completed until the 17th and 18th centuries. As a result of this transformation Turin assumed its peculiar urban character–part Italian, part French–and combined austerity with elegance. The city reached the apex of its historical importance in the 19th century, when it became the political and moral center of the Risorgimento, and between 1861 and 1865 had the privilege of being Italy's first national capital.

Page 74

Top Panoramic view of the center of Turin, ringed by the Alps.

Page 74 bottom

Piazza San Carlo is surrounded by Baroque façades, elegant mansions and arcades. In the center is the monument to Emanuele Filiberto of Savoy (1520-1580).

Page 75

The Sardinian Army monument, opposite the Palazzo Madama, lit by the warm light of the setting sun.

Pages 76-77

An unusual image of Emanuele Filiberto of Savoy (1520-1580) monument, seen above the colorful crowd and activities of a public holiday.

Page 78
The Mole Antonelliana, built in 1863 by Alessandro Antonelli, is the emblem of Turin.

Pages 78-79
The River Po passes to the south of Turin, creating handsome panoramic vistas and their evocative reflections.

The city offers a very special hidden itinerary through old shops and elegant meeting places where visitors can still fully enjoy the sober, refined atmosphere of "Old Turin." Via Roma, Galleria San Federico and Galleria Subapina also have antiquarian bookshops and shops devoted to numismatic pursuits, while Piazza San Carlo, Via Po and Via Maria Vittoria are home to exquisite goldsmiths' workshops. The traditional Turinese art of confectionery still lives on in the period confectionery shops and historic cafés like Baratti, in which one can savor all the memories of the Belle Epoque.

Pages 82-83
The skillfully illuminated Piazza Castello is one of Turin's most crowded evening meeting places.

Vercelli
Under gothic spires

Vercelli's layout dates principally from the 18th and 19th centuries and is characterized by spacious tree-lined boulevards with Neo-Classic buildings and Art Nouveau villas. The splendid Basilica of Sant'Andrea clearly reflects the city's prosperity in the period of the Free Cities, as do the civic towers and bell-towers, like the one adjacent to the Cathedral, which dates from the 12th century. In 1427 Vercelli passed from the Viscontis' control to that of Amedeus VIII of Savoy. Dating from the Renaissance period is the courtyard of Palazzo dei Centori, inspired by Brunelleschi, and Gaudenzio Ferrari's frescoes in the church of San Cristoforo, as well as the austere Savoy fortress, now the seat of Vercelli's courts.

Page 87 top
The Basilica of Sant'Andrea is one of the earliest examples of Cistercian-type Gothic architecture in Italy. Built between 1219 and 1227, it is one of the most significant medieval buildings in Piedmont.

Pages 86-87
Piazza Cavour, the characteristic city center, is completely surrounded by arcades. Above the houses emerge the octagonal Torre dell'Angelo and Torre di Città, which both date from the Medieval period.

**Aosta
Standard of the
Roman Empire**

Pages 90-91
The mountain ranges offer magical perspectives for an exhilarating flight.

Aosta was founded by the Romans in 25 B.C. in honor of Augustus. In the course of the centuries the city became adorned with remarkable monuments, of which imposing traces remain. During the early Middle Ages the city was much fought over, but in the 11th century it fell definitively under the House of Savoy's control. Since World War II, the city has undergone remarkable development, but without losing its mountain-village charm and keeping intact its typical rustic atmosphere, together with its craft and folkloristic traditions.

Genoa
The heirs of Andrea Doria

The Maritime Republic of Genoa gained control of the Tyrrhenian Sea between the 11th and 14th centuries and spread its colonies, emporiums, and ports-of-call from Corsica to North Africa, from the Aegean Islands to Syria, and on as far as the distant Crimea. The independence of this glorious republic lasted until the Napoleonic period, when it was annexed to Piedmont in 1814. For the arts the two most prolific periods were the Middle Ages and the 16th and 17th centuries. In the compact nucleus formed by the old quarters (which stretch out between the Port, Via Garibaldi and Piazza De Ferrari and are characterized by the maze of narrow alleyways) Genoa's most significant monuments are to be found.

Page 92

Santa Maria Assunta in Carignano is one of the city's largest churches and reflects a particularly rich and magnificent Baroque style.

Page 93

Via Garibaldi; attractive reflections in the windows of Palazzo Rosso, another example of Baroque architecture.

Pages 94-95

True metropolis of the Ligurian region, Genoa is the largest commercial port in Italy and among the largest in the Mediterranean.

Page 96

The delights of the Genoan cuisine are well known to gourmets: pesto, torta pasqualina, focaccia all'olio, "musciame"and "gianchetti" are but some of the many specialities.

Pages 96-97

The characteristic narrow streets, known as carugi, are often no more than 5 feet wide and are lined with old buildings that may rise eight stories.

Boccadasse gives the impression that time has stood still. This old seaside village has kept intact its typical houses with their painted façades, and there are boats beached on the sand. Faces scorched by sun and salt tell the secrets of the sea, the fishermen speak the straightforward and authentic language of maritime uses and traditions. Bocadasse is in a central position vis à vis the new part of the city, but has not been contaminated by its expansion and has managed to maintain its charm unaltered.

Pages 100-101
Sunset is the moment in which Genoa most clearly shows off that particular beauty which has earned her the title of "La Superba."

Trento
The city of the
Prince-Bishops

Pages 104-105
A close-up of Fogolino's beautiful fresco on Case Rella. Together with his brother, Fogolino also worked on the Magno Palazzo Clesiano.

Pages 102-103
Panoramic view of the historic city center.

Page 102 top
In Piazza Duomo; the frescoes on the façades of the 16th-century houses known as "Case Rella" are by the Venetian artist Fogolino.

Page 103 top
The cathedral complex retains a finely preserved medieval appearance.

Page 103 bottom
A detail of Piazza Duomo, the city's historic center.

Of Roman origin, Trento became was the seat of an episcopal principality in the Middle Ages and many of its art and architectural works, mainly churches, date from that period. During the Renaissance the city experienced a remarkable renewal, principally due to its humanistic prince-bishop, Bernardo Clesio. The inner city, compressed between the cathedral and the Castello del Buonconsiglio (the two historic centers of power), reflects a noble and restrained architecture.

Page 106 top

The Magno Palazzo Clesiano occupies part of the Castello del Buonconsiglio. Among its treasures is the sumptuous Loggia del Romanino, one of the finest examples of Italian 15th-century mural painting.

Page 106 bottom

The trident-bearing god Neptune dominates the water spouts of the lovely Baroque fountain at the center of Piazza Duomo. The fountain dates from 1786.

Page 107

The Cathedral bell-tower culminates in a massive onion-shaped cupola. This architectural motif, common in religious building throughout northern Europe, bears witness to the historic relationship between Trento and the Holy Roman Empire.

Venice
Inlaid in marble

The particular atmosphere of Venice is a singular combination of eternal changelessness and insidious changeability. The city's mood changes with the weather, the seasons and the time of day. A natural protagonist, the city likes to present herself in ever-changing ways to amaze and bewilder any who fool themselves into thinking they have definitively understood her. She stubbornly refuses any definition that imprisons her in a fixed scheme, delighting every day in being the exact opposite of herself.

Page 108 top

The city's profile stands out clearly on the horizon of the lagoon.

Page 108 bottom

The traditional ironwork known as a pettine decorates the prows of the gondolas moored at the San Marco landing stage.

Page 109

In 1562, the Venetian Senate ordered that all gondolas be painted black.

Pages 110-111

For centuries the winged lion has been the symbol of the La Serenissima.

Pages 112-113

The Rialto Bridge, created in 1180 as a bridge of barges, was not built in stone until 1591. It was designed by Antonio da Ponte.

Pages 114-115

Venice is inconceivable without its gondoliers who, with their typical straw hats, control their vessels from the stern with a single oar.

Pages 116-117

The Sala delle Quattro Porte, inside the Doge's Palace, was designed by Antonio da Ponte.

For richness and mobility of color and light, for ever-changing perspectives, and the beauty of their elegant architectural formulations, the Venetian palazzi offer an unforgettable sight. The marble palaces of the ancient Venetian nobility, whose coats of arms are painted on the mooring posts along the front of the residences, date from the 12th to the 17th century. Some exhibit a flowering of Gothic art and characteristic pointed arches that intertwine to form aerial lace-work; Renaissance palaces, with their harmonious loggias and arches and rich and ornate Baroque balconies stand side by side with sober Classic-style palaces; and typically Venetian-Byzantine constructions and the frescoed façades of 14th-century palaces stand should to shoulder–all in a sumptuous mixture of styles.

Page 118

In the darkness of the night the asymmetric façade of Ca'Dario shines out. This early Renaissance gem dates from 1487.

Pages 118-119

The historic buildings are reflected on the polished decking of a gondola as it crosses the lagoon.

Page 119 top

Every glimpse and every image reveals the city's inexhaustible artistic richness.

Pages 120-121

The historic heart of Venice faces onto the broad St. Mark's Basin, at the center of which is the Island of San Giorgio.

Verona
Between arches and squares the profile of Juliet

Page 122 top

Gracing the courtyard of a 13th-century palace, Juliet's balcony is the destination of thousands of tourists.

Page 122 bottom

Piazza Dante is surrounded by the Baroque-style Domus Nova and the Renaissance-style Loggia del Consiglio.

Pages 122-123

Castelvecchio was the second and last residence of the Scaligeri family.

Page 123 top left

The panorama of Verona is rendered even more beautiful by the gently flowing Adige and traces of the city's noble medieval past.

Page 123 top right

The Arena, built in the 1st century A.D., is the setting for a world-famous opera festival.

Verona enjoyed importance and prosperity in Roman times thanks to its strategic position in northern Italy. In the early Middle Ages its role remained undiminished as it was often the seat of post-Roman rulers, but in the 13th and 14th centuries Verona's importance increased both as a Free City and then one under the powerful and ambitious Scaligeri family's dominion. Its noble, sacred and secular buildings date from this period. In 1404 Verona came under the Venetian sphere of influence and remained tied to this city until 1796. During this period it became a lively artistic center with an illustrious school of painting in which artists such as Pisanello and Veronese were active.

Page 124

The frescoes on Casa dei Mazzanti in Piazza delle Erbe were created by Alberto Cavalli in the 16th century.

Page 125

The Torre Lamberti reflected alluringly in a window in the city center.

Pages 128-129
The luminous charm of the Giusti Garden, embellished with fountains, statues, and a wooded labyrinth.

Verona is remarkably rich in both color and in characteristic quiet corners. Piazza delle Erbe, on the site of the ancient Roman Forum, is the true heart of the city. It is surrounded by ancient buildings and towers, and the characteristic umbrellas of the daily market add a lively picturesque note.

In the center of the square, alongside the 14th-century Colonna del Mercato, is a splendid 16th-century marble aedicule. Among the palaces, the 14th-century Casa dei Mercanti, with its mullioned windows and crenellation, and the imposing Baroque-style Palazzo Maffei stand out.

Padua
University goliardy

Of all the major cities of the Venetian region, Padua, although possessing outstanding works of art, is perhaps the city with the least monumental appearance. Despite its rather irregular topography, the old quarters with their long, arcaded streets abound in picturesque corners. Life in Padua is very vibrant and the many university students are a distinctive feature throughout the city. The University keeps Padua's cultural prestige high, and the extremely rich artistic heritage of the city's numerous churches and museums and other initiatives help to nourish it.

Page 130
Celebrations and joy on graduation day.

Pages 130-131
The Church of Santa Giustina is a grandiose structure surmounted by a complex of eight cupolas. In the background is the Basilica of Sant'Antonio.

Page 131 top left
The Caffè Petrocchi, the historic meeting place of 19th-century literary figures, remains a reference point in Padua's social life.

Page 131 top right
Piazza delle Erbe is surrounded by old porticoed houses, among which Palazzo della Ragione stands out.

Page 132

The Prato della Valle (Meadow of the Valley) is an expansive open space at whose center rises a garden, gracefully adorned with statues and encircled by a canal.

Page 133

At the back of Piazza dei Signori is the former Palazzo del Capitano, whose façade, designed by Falconetto in 1523, incorporates the Arco dell'Orologio (the Clock Arch). The clock, the first in Italy, dates back to 1437.

Trieste
Habsburgian memories

Pages 136-137
Piazza Unità d'Italia opens onto the seafront and is the center of life in Trieste. Built at the end of the 18th century, it is embellished with magnificent buildings.

Pages 134-135
Riva Tre Novembre parallels the seafront for a good distance and draws a large part of the city's traffic.

Page 134 top
The Grand Canal, which flows into the sea to the north of the port of Trieste, was dug in 1756.

Page 135 top left
The crowded fish market plays an important role in the city's life.

Page 135 top right
The cafés are well frequented; a number have long-standing historical and cultural traditions.

Page 135 bottom
Miramare Castle, built for Maximilian of Austria, is one of the finest examples of a princely residence of the 1750-1800 period.

Udine
The dignity of the past

Udine superseded Cividale as the most important center of the Friuli region in 1238, when the Patriarch Bertolo moved the Patriarchal Seat there from Aquileia. A few towers of the long-gone city walls, the churches of Santa Maria in Castello and San Francesco and a part of the Cathedral are all that remain from the medieval period. The most characteristic areas of the city center date principally from the first period of Venetian dominion. In this period the city's layout was renewed and embellished with many buildings and monuments in the Gothic and Renaissance styles tempered by Venetian inspiration. In the 18th century, the painter Tiepolo's genius added to the city's cultural heritage.

Top
Via del Municipio is the meeting place for Udine's youth, and the most popular street for the traditional *passeggiata*.

Pages 138-139
The Loggia del Lionello in Piazza della Libertà was designed by Niccolò Lionelli and built between 1448-1456.

Page 139 top left
The statue of Justice, flanked by two bronze Moors, crowns the roof of the Clock Tower.

Page 139 top right
The San Giovanni arcade in Piazza della Libertà is dominated by the Clock Tower.

Pages 140-141
Two bronze Moors and a statue representing Justice enliven the roof of the Torre dell'Orologio.

Today, Udine is a lively city which combines its traditional function as Friuli's administrative and commercial center with many industrial activities. Numerous cultural institutions, such as the Friulian Philological Society and the Academy of the Arts and Literature also flourish. Udine's rich cultural heritage is maintained in the Civic Library, housed in a noble Palladian palace, as well as in the Gallery of Ancient and Modem Art and the Natural History Museum.

Pages 142-143
The monument to the Treaty of Campoformio (1797) and a 16th-century fountain enliven Piazza della Libertà and offer passersby unexpectedly peaceful retreats.

Bologna
Imposing and compact

Bologna boasts Etruscan and Roman origins and experienced an intense cultural life, especially in the 11th and 12th centuries. It was one of the first municipalities to declare itself a "Free City" and, after the wars against the Holy Roman Emperors Frederick I Barbarossa and Frederick II, reached the apogee of its fortunes. Factional strife led to the dominion of various families and eventually the city passed definitively into the power of the Church, where it remained until 1859. When it was a Free City, Bologna's famous university, which attracted students from all parts of Europe, enjoyed its greatest prestige. The city's monumental appearance derives from the Renaissance period, with works by architects and artists such as Vignola, Jacopo della Quercia, Michelangelo, and Giambologna.

Page 144 top
The slightly leaning Asinelli and Garisenda towers, built in the 11th and 12th centuries, have been chosen to symbolize Bologna.

Pages 144-145
The stupendous cloister of Santo Stefano's Basilica, with two loggias in different architectural styles, dates from the 10th and 13th centuries.

Page 145 top
The Gothic Basilica of San Petronio, Palazzo del Podestà, Palazzo Comunale, and Palazzo dei Banchi bound the noble Piazza Maggiore, Bolgona's center.

Page 145 bottom
Bologna's skyline is pierced by medieval towers, notably the leaning Asinelli and Garisenda towers and the Arengo tower.

Pages 146-147
Via Rizzoli, one of the main thoroughfares in the city, leads into Piazza Ravegnana, where the stand-alone Asinelli and Garisenda towers rise.

Page 148 left

The tomb of Rolandino de' Passeggeri dominates the square in front of the Basilica of San Domenico.

Page 148 top right

The market is characteristic of traditional Bologna.

Page 148 bottom right

Everyday life captured in the streets of the city center.

Page 149

This aerial view of Bologna reveals city's splendid urban structure, in which the new has been integrated into the old.

Ravenna
The city-mosaic

Ravenna was capital of the Western Roman Empire in the 5th and 6th centuries and the point of contact between the Byzantine and the Roman worlds. Galla Placidia, Odoacer and Theodoric embellished it with superb buildings including the Mausoleum of Galla Placidia, the Basilica of San Vitale, the Baptistery, Sant'Appollinare Nuovo and

Sant'Apollinare in Classe. These structures form the most significant record of the transition of Christian architecture and art from the Classic to the Byzantine styles. Ravenna's churches have a characteristic external form: the apse is polygonal and the interior is illuminated by marvelous mosaic decorations, unique in the world.

Page 150
The stupendous mosaics on the walls and ceiling of San Vitale present scenes from the New Testament.

Page 151
The original core of the Church of St. John the Evangelist dates from the 5th century; the austere portal is in Gothic style.

A great contrast exists in Ravenna between the city's general appearance and its group of Early Christian and Byzantine monuments, which appear to be isolated in a timeless dimension. The Ravenna of the characteristic cylindrical bell-towers, erected in the 9th and 10th centuries, lives side by side with the Renaissance city that is the result restructuring by the Venetians in 1400. In the last 20 years, as a result of a rapid industrial growth, Ravenna has added a modern sector, particularly in the Porto Corsini zone. Ravenna's cultural activities are nourished by its unrivaled patrimony of Roman, Byzantine and Medieval antiquities, of which its museums have first-class collections.

Parma
The city with a past as a small capital

After having played a major role during the Roman Empire and as a Free City, Parma's period of splendor began in 1545 when the city became the capital of the Farnese family's duchy. When walking through Parma's central streets, squares and ducal park, it is still possible to feel the dignified nobility of the ur-ban layout. The city's past is documented not only by monuments but also by rich cultural traditions kept alive by the University, by numerous art collections including that of the National Gallery, and by a passion for music. In fact, the audience attending the Teatro Regio is one of the most demanding and critical in Italy.

Page 154
Via Pisacane opens out onto the Cathedral's lofty Gothic bell-tower, characterized by mullioned windows, and the octagonal Baptistery, embellished by loggias and distinctive architraves.

Pages 154-155
After-dark lighting confers an alluring atmosphere on Piazza Garibaldi's dignified elegance.

Page 155 top left
The historic pharmacy of St. John the Baptist was originally founded between the 9th and 10th centuries, and once run by Benedictine monks.

Page 155 top right
The 17th-century Palazzo del Governatore is in Piazza Garibaldi, in the center of the city.

Page 157
A detail of the Cathedral cupola's magnificent frescoes, painted by Correggio between 1526 and 1530.

Page 156 top
The Renaissance church of St. John the Evangelist has a splendid library.

Page 156 bottom
The Baptistery is one of the finest examples of Italian Romanesque sculpture, especially in its niches and the decorative fascias, which are the work of Benedetto Antelami.

Modena
A duchy far from the metropolises

Modena's encircling walls enclose an urban space within which the architecture of streets and buildings recalls the splendor and historical events of the old city, then known as Mutina. The large Romanesque cathedral, built in light-colored stone, represents the medieval world, but Modena's most evocative traces are without doubt from the period when the city was ruled by the Este family, which had its court there in the 16th and 17th centuries. Even today, artistic and historical elements and ancient gastronomic traditions live side by side and make Modena the capital of "good living."

Pages 160-161

The aerial view of Modena illustrates the regular plan of the Roman urbs. Beside the cathedral can be seen the Ghirlandina Tower with its slender Gothic spire.

Florence
A Concert of Arts

Florentia was founded as a Roman colony in 59 B.C. in the area between the Arno and the Mugnone rivers. Under Emperor Hadrian the original nucleus of the city began to grow, and the first bridge over the Arno was built. The year 1000 marked the start of Florence's ascent, and by 1300 the city had become the most important cultural center in Italy, home to Giotto and Dante. The "modern" city was shaped during the Renaissance thanks to the Medici, who welcomed to their court such artists as Brunelleschi, Donatello, Masaccio, and Paolo Uccello, who contributed to the now incalculable artistic wealth of Florence.

Page 162

Two different ways to experience Florence: the marvels of the museums or a peaceful spot on the Ponte Vecchio.

Page 163

The façade of Santa Maria Novella reflects the Renaissance genius of Leon Battista Alberti. Entirely surfaced with polychromatic marble it comes together in two volutes before culminating in an incredibly beautiful tympanum adorned with wonderful inlays.

Pages 164-165

The complete system of volumes and mass in Brunelleschi's cupola culminates in the marble lantern, the focal point of the entire edifice.

Pages 166-167

The goldsmiths' workshops on the Ponte Vecchio, glimpsed during a snowfall, look like something from an Impressionist painting.

Page 169 top left
With its elegant polychromatic decoration, the profile of Giotto's bell-tower stands out in the city panorama.

Page 169 top right
Rising up in the background is the outstandingly massive structure of the Baptistery, one of the oldest buildings in Florence.

Pages 168-169
The Boboli Gardens represent a precious example of a typical Italian garden. As from the top of an imaginary Mt. Olympus, visitors can admire evocative views of the city center.

Pages 170-171
Dusk fading over Piazzale Michelangelo; the clamor of the crowd is now far away.

Pages 172-173
The unmistakable structures on Ponte Vecchio are reflected in the Arno as the city's night life begins to liven up.

Pisa
Marble Wonders

Pisa, already an important naval base in Roman times, reached the height of its splendor in the Middle Ages. Its period of prosperity and achievement in the arts continued under the rule of the Grand Dukes of Tuscany, and in the sciences, Galileo Galilei was the author of fiercely challenged theories and founded a scientific tradition valid to this day. The city gradually grew in size, taking on its modern look and adding industrial and commercial activities to pre-existing functions. However, Pisa's historic center still remains its heart, both a meeting place and a crossing point.

Pages 174-175
It is difficult to describe the "miracle" that Pisa offers to visitors, thanks to possessing one of the most beautiful squares in the world. The surrounding lawns highlight the blinding freshness of four marble gems: The Camposanto, the Baptistery, the Cathedral, and the Leaning Tower.

Page 176 top

It is a common belief that Palazzo dell'Orologio rises up on the ruins of the Torre della Muda or della Fame, (of Hunger) sadly renowned for the death of Conte Ugolino and immortalized in Dante's Inferno.

Page 176 bottom

The Church of Santa Maria della Spina, a precious gem of Romanesque-Gothic architecture owes its name to the fact that it once contained a thorn from Christ's crown.

Pages 176-177

The setting sun pinkens the historic buildings on Lungo Arno Pacinotti.

While the Arno winds silently through the city, artificial lights try to compete with the twilight's warm tones. Its important historical and artistic traditions make Pisa an unusually fascinating city. An air of serene decorum wafts out from Piazza dei Miracoli and pervades the entire city.

Siena
A return to the Middle Ages

Medieval Siena is not just Piazza del Campo and the Cathedral or Via di Città and the Baptistery. As well as the individual monuments for which it is justly famous, Siena draws its charm from its silent, narrow streets that climb and descend tortuously but sinuously. The marked differences in height of the different parts of the city create views and scenes of surprising beauty, framing the Torre del Mangia and the Cathedral from several sides, against a backdrop of valleys and slopes. The town's remarkable history comes to life with every step.

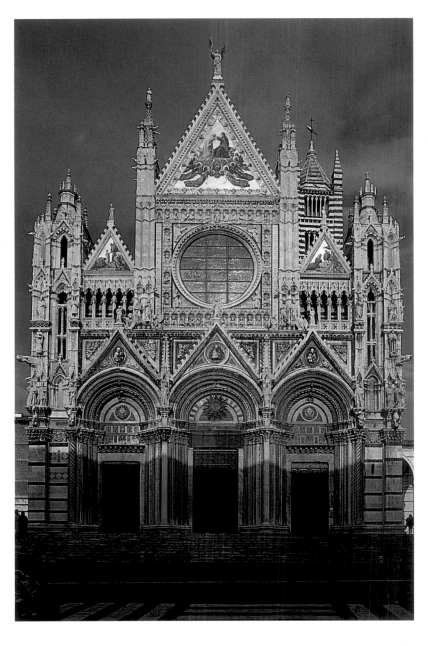

Pages 182-183
In the dense medieval lay-out, the houses are built along narrow streets which follow the winding contours of the areas of high ground on which the city is built.

Pages 184-185
The slender Torre del Mangia and the Palazzo Pubblico cast their shadows into the magnificent Piazza del Campo.

The origins of the Palio date back to the 16th century. On 2 July 1597, a Medici soldier fired an arquebus shot at an effigy of the Madonna. To make amends for such a sacrilege a church was built and a Palio organized. Ever since then, on 2 July and 16 August, the Palio is contested amid an extraordinary flaring up of enthusiasm and popular passion. After a procession of the inhabitants of the city's various quarters, in which the participants wear splendid medieval costumes, the fierce horse race, with relentlessly goaded mounts, begins in Piazza del Campo.

Perugia
Municipal Nobility

Perugia's origins are lost in the mists of time. The hills on which the city rises were already inhabited in prehistoric times when the volcanoes of Monte Amiata were still active. The urban layout is a typical example of an Etruscan and Roman city that has gradually expanded to reach a new circle of walls.

There are few cities which deserve to be visited street by street and building by building as does Perugia: Palazzo dei Priori, the Umbrian National Gallery, the Cathedral of San Lorenzo and the famous Fontana Maggiore are but a few of the many hundred masterpieces to be admired.

Pages 190-191

The Umbrian hills take on a rosy hue at sunset and time seems to stand still.

Pages 192-193

The city emerges from a misty horizon and the labyrinth of small streets appears polished by the rain.

**Assisi
The city which speaks
with heaven**

Assisi is built of white and pink Subasio stone laid on top of manmade terraces. The steep, narrow streets often consist of flights of steps. Assisi's medieval structure combined with its many artistic merits make it one of Italy's most intact and authentic historic cities. The vivid memories of St. Francis and the gently sloping countryside around it make it Assisi one of those rare places steeped in spirituality. Yet the true face of the town can be found in some secluded comer or in those rare moments when streets and squares are not crowded with visitors.

Page 196

Among the churches of Assisi, the one dedicated to San Rufino, its patron saint, deserves pride of place in art history for its typical Romanesque façade, divided into three horizontal zones by two lines of pendent arches.

Page 197

The Basilica of St. Francis is composed of two churches, one above the other. Visitors enter the lower church through a Gothic-style portal beneath a finely worked rose window.

Naples
A Palette of Sounds
and Colors

Page 198
Chaotic traffic is a constant characteristic of Naples' inner-city streets.

Pages 198-199
The picturesque inlet of Mergellina is one of Naples' most celebrated spots.

Page 199 top
The blue Neapolitan Gulf and the cone of Vesuvius always exercise a certain inexplicable charm on the viewer.

Pages 200

The precise lines of the Royal Palace define the spacious Piazza del Plebiscito. Since the 17th century the palace has lodged Spanish viceroys, Austrian princes, Bourbon kings, and most recently, the royal house of Savoy.

Page 201

At Christmas, in keeping with tradition, the Christ Child in the Manger is displayed in the elegant setting of the Galleria Umberto I (1887-1891), designed by Emanuele Rocco.

Il presepe è stato
allestito
dal Maestro
Luigi Signore

COMUNE DI NAPOLI

Il presepe del maestro Luigi Signore
è patrocinato dal Comune di Napoli

To grasp Naples' true spirit visitors must walk through the traditional inner-city neighborhoods and observe the vitality and the cunning of the street urchins and the petty traffickers, listen to the singing voices of the market traders, mingle with the gesticulating crowd which invades streets, lanes and squares at all hours, and let themselves be carried away by the exuberance and animation so typical of the Neapolitan soul. A large part of the population of these bassi (slums) carry on their private lives in the courtyards and the lanes. The true sceneggiata originates from this spontaneous folklore and is rendered inimitable by the use of dialect.

Pages 204-205

Castello Capuano, a gray rectangular building, is now the seat of the law courts. It was built by the Normans and later enlarged by the Swabians. The Castello was a royal palace until 1400, when the Aragonese moved to Castello Nuovo. The Normans, Swabians, and Aragonese were successive foreign overlords.

Page 206 top

Life in Naples is characterized by a certain religiousness, and it is still possible to find workshops in which craftsmen restore and make all sorts of sacred effigies.

Page 206 bottom

Fishermen preparing their nets in the calm waters of the port.

Pages 206-207

A drive in a horse-driven carriage is an attractive way of getting to know the city.

Bari
Terminus for the
Orient

Page 210
Beautiful images of the port, with early morning work under way.

Pages 210-211
An aerial view of the city.

Pages 212-123
The Petruzzelli Theater is one of the temples of Italian bel canto. Every year the best-known performers of the international opera world perform here.

The contrast between the urban layout and living conditions of the old and the modern city is striking. The former, concentrated in the area between the old and the new ports, has a typical medieval layout with narrow, winding streets; the latter is based on a rational town-planning scheme and is characterized by major facilities constructed for the city's commercial and industrial development. Today Naples is a primary entrepôt for trade in the lower Adriatic and with the East.

Page 214
The strong religious feeling of Bari's inhabitants has left its traces in many aspects of public life, especially in the older part of the city.

Page 215
Rising up like a lighthouse, the Cathedral's bell tower dominates the Old Port.

Matera
The city which
emerges from the rock

This very individual city consists of a modern part which extends over a plain and an old part situated around the edge and on the steep slopes of a hill. The structure of the historic core has remained almost intact over the centuries: steep streets and lanes, often with flights of stairs, climb up the hill past houses hollowed out of the tuff. These constructions, which open up like large eyes dug out of the mountain, create an atmosphere which is sometimes mysterious and unnerving and other times very evocative.

Page 216
A foggy image of Matera in winter.

Page 217
An evening view of the city.

The most picturesque aspect of Matera is the "Sassi" houses situated in a disorderly fashion down the hillside. For the most part they have been dug out like grottoes in successive levels in the calcareous cliff. The panorama is disconcerting, and on sunny days the glare of the stones of the old city is emphasized and it looks like a village in Asia Minor.

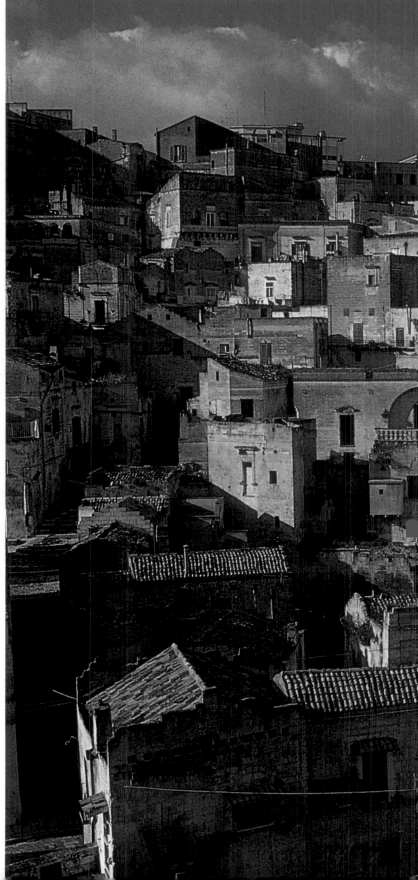

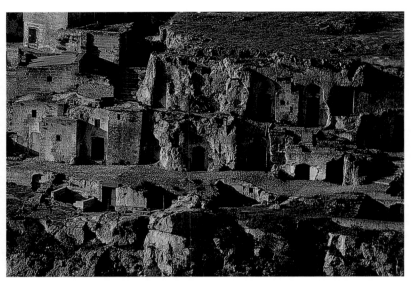

Palermo
The Arab-Norman
Capital

Pages 220-221

Palermo palpitates with light under the pink veil of sunset.

Page 221 top

The elaborate pinnacles of the Church of Santa Rosalia and the Moorish-style cloister of the Church of San Giovanni degli Eremiti create an oriental image.

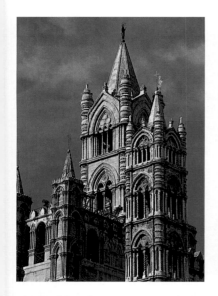

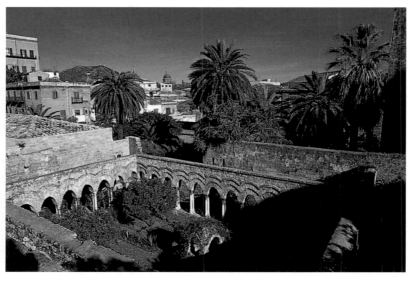

The city presents itself to visitors as animated and joyful in its splendid natural setting. The voices and the clamor of the market mingle with the cheerful confusion of people who crowd the inner city's tortuous, narrow streets, creating a typical scene of the everyday life of the ordinary people.

Palermo was a Phoenician, Roman and Byzantine city as well as the capital of Sicily under Arab dominion. Under Norman dominion, around the middle of the 13th century, it reached the height of its wealth and artistic and cultural splendor. This medley of historical events and the passage of different peoples led to the construction of splendid buildings and the fusion of Arab, Byzantine and Latin elements, which gives the city a very special charm.

Page 224 top

The cupolas of the Church of San Giovanni degli Eremiti recall those of a mosque.

Page 224 bottom

The magnificent stonework detailing on the façade of the Basilica of Santa Rosalia.

Page 225

The Basilica of Santa Rosalia is one of the city's most imposing and picturesque building. It was constructed in 1185 but underwent various structural changes until 1804.

Pages 226-227

As though in a phantasmagorical scene, the marble figures of the Pretoria Fountain seem to come alive with the arrival of darkness.

Catania
The city in the shadow of the volcano

The origins of Catania date back to the 7th century B.C. when it developed as a Greek colony. Later, both under the Roman Empire and in the Middle Ages, it enjoyed a particularly rich period of economic and artistic growth. Catania is situated on Sicily's eastern coast, below the southern flank of Etna. It is a magnificent site on a fertile plain, on which citrus fruits are grown. Thanks to its numerous 17th-century Baroque buildings, the city presents a noble and sumptuous presence. However, the disastrous earthquake of 1693, the eruptions of Etna, and damage caused during World War II destroyed much of the artistic heritage that the city had conserved from preceding eras. Around Catania's magnificent 17th-century core, modern expansion has led to development of industrial zones.

Pages 228-229

The gardens, green spaces and luxuriant palm trees of Catania's squares offer a refreshing resting place when the heat reaches its height.

Page 229 top

The imposing façade of a building in the city center.

Page 230

A sunny image of Catania, situated between Etna and the sea.

Pages 230-231

In a curious juxtaposition, Baroque cupolas and Etna's snow-clad summit both lie beneath the glaring Sicilian sun.

Cagliari
A basin of light

Cagliari is lively and modern. The sunny, luminous city is studded with large green spaces divided by busy boulevards and heavily trafficked roads. Together with Via Roma, the Terrazza Umberto I (also called the Bastion of St. Remy), is one of the spots most frequented by young people. Situated on the old 15th-century Spanish bastions, the terrace offers magnificent views of the city neighborhoods below and the gulf beyond.

Page 232
A symbolic representation of the victory of Faith over Heresy: a lion brings down a bull in this sculpture at the foot of the presbytery steps in Cagliari Cathedral.

Pages 232-233
The Umberto I terrace offers unrivaled panoramas over Cagliari. It overlooks the historic city center, the gulf, and the hills that surround Sardinia's handsome capital.

Page 233 top left
In the background is the hemicycle on the Umberto I terrace. A late addition to the city's 16th-century Spanish ramparts, the hemicycle was built between 1899 and 1902.

Page 233 top right
Two lunettes inspired by Byzantine mosaics adorn the façade of Cagliari cathedral.

Pages 234-235
Crowds of young people brighten the streets of central Cagliari until late in the evening.

Page 236 top

In the highest part of the city is the old Castello, whose bastions and towers reveal their Spanish inspiration.

Pages 236-237

Despite Cagliari's industrial and commercial character, a flight of pink flamingoes over the saltwater lagoons suggests an uncontaminated natural environment.

Page 237 top

Currently, life in Cagliari revolves around the activity of the port, the natural outlet to Campidiano, the richest zone in Sardinia.

Pages 238-239
The setting sun illuminates Cagliari with thousands of pinkish hues.

Page 240
Verona: mythological figures as in a Garden of Venus.

Thanks have to be extended in particular to:
Gianni and Giuliana Biggio, Bruno Quaranta, Luisa Tschabushnig, Azienda Autonoma di Promozione Turistica of Palermo, Azienda Autonoma di Promozione Turistica of Catania, Regione Lombardia, Terrazza Martini of Milan.

Photographic References

Marcello Bertinetti:
Back-cover, pages 1, 2-3, 4-5, 6-7, 8-9, 10-11, 12-13, 15, 16-17; Rome: pages 22-39; Milan: page 50, page 55 top right, page 57 bottom; Turin: pages 74-83; Vercelli: pages 84-87; Genoa: pages 92-101; Trento: pages 102-107; Venice: pages 108-121; Bari: pages 211; Cagliari: pages 232-239.

Giulio Veggi:
Cover, pages 14, 18-19, 20, 21; Milan: pages 40-51, pages 54-57; Varese: pages 58-61; Bergamo: pages 62-65; Como: pages 66-69; Verona: pages 122-129; Padua: pages 130-133; Trieste: pages 134-137; Udine: pages 138-143; Bologna: pages 144-149; Ravenna: pages 150-153; Parma: pages 154-157; Florence: pages 162-165, pages 168-173; Pisa: pages 174-179; Siena: pages 180-185; Perugia:

pages 188-193; Assisi: pages 194-197; Naples: pages 198-209; Bari: pages 210, 212-215; Matera: pages 216-219; Palermo: pages 220-227; Catania: pages 228-231; page 240.

Francesco Paolo Cito:
Siena: pages 186-187.

Lelli e Masotti/Photographic Archive of Teatro alla Scala of Milan:
Milan: pages 52-53.

Franco Nucci:
Florence: pages 166-167.

Luciano Ramires:
Aosta: pages 88-91.

Ghigo Roli:
Mantua: pages 70-73; Modena: pages 158-161.